Chackra
for beginners

Introduction to Healing Power and Oriental Relaxation Techniques and Healing

By : **Pamela Wilford**
First edition: July 2022
Copyright © 2022 : Pamela Wilford

Copyright

3

Limited Liability - Exclusion of Liability

INDEX

Introduction

If you've ever practiced yoga or learned about Eastern spirituality, or even if you're only familiar with a few pop culture references, you've probably already heard of the chakras. And *at least* you will know that the chakras are energy centers connected to certain parts of the body and the subtle energy that moves through them.

This book is an introduction to a topic of greater complexity. It is neither an exhaustive account of the chakras, nor the only account of the chakras. Although they may be known by other names, chakra-like systems, subtle body maps, are found in many spiritual cultures and traditions, from Indian Hinduism and Buddhist vajrayana, to Chinese Taoism, Western esotericism, and even Kabbalah.

But in this book, we will focus on the Hindu system of the seven chakras. It is not the only chakra system, nor is it the only Hindu chakra system. Any number of chakras has been affected: five, six, seven, twenty and even more. So to say that the situation is complicated is an understatement.

There is also a debate about whether the different chakra systems should be descriptions of a real subtle body with real energy centers similar to physical organs, or whether they were simply intended as guides to visualize different types of meditation.

Even so, in this book, we will treat the chakras *as if* they were real components of a southern body, even when we leave unanswered the general question of their existential state (physical?, psychic?, imaginary?, fictitious?). This agnostic approach means that you don't have to believe in the literal reality of the chakras to get something out of this book and start working with the chakra system.

If you're interested in chakras in the first place, you're probably doing some sort of spiritual practice, like yoga. But to start with the chakras, you don't have to buy any particular religious point of view. You don't even have to believe that chakras exist. All you need is an openness to experimentation and the ability to use your imagination.

The general idea of any chakra system is this: your body has a number of energy channels or *nadis*, some of them major and others minor. Different types of subtle energy (*vayu* or "wind") move through these channels, which affect both the body and mind. The points where the channels intersectin the body are called chakras (literally "wheels"). There are many chakras in the body, but the best-known system outlines seven main chakras.

This subtle energy system is prone to imbalances that can cause both large and small physical, emotional, and spiritual disturbances. In particular, the chakras are vulnerable to blockages and overexcitement, so they need to be balanced. When the seven chakras are open, the free flow of energy through them causes spiritual awakening.

The idea of a subtle energy system in the body dates back to the Upanishads of the 7th or 8th century BC, but the chakra system began to take its familiar form only later, in the tantric period. There are many misconceptions about tantra in the West, mainly the idea that it's all about sex. But tantra is not so much about better sex or a better orgasm than working with one's own embodied experience rather than trying to transcend the body, using the senses as a means of awakening spirituality rather than trying to block the senses. It involves a huge literature and a huge body of meditative and yogic techniques, of which only a fraction involves sexuality.

The main thing among the ideas of tantra is that the universe is the manifestation of the ultimate divine reality. This means in chakra terms is that your body is a microcosm of the larger universe, and the divine energy manifested by the iris also acts in the body of the individual practitioner.

Working with the chakras can be tremendously liberating, but this approach is not without its dangers. Among other things, it can have undesirable effects on your psychological well-being. This is why practices involving the subtle body are traditionally done with the close guidance of a qualified spiritual teacher who can correct any mistakes made by a student, see the blind spots of his ego and help him stay away from common dangers and solve any problems that may arise. So, if you find yourself wanting to enter the chakras more deeply as a result of reading this book, I highly recommend that you find a teacher who can guide you in your practice.

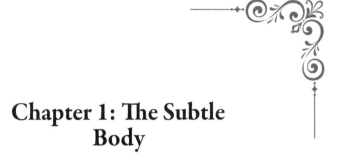

Chapter 1: The Subtle Body

If you've spent a significant amount of time on the meditation pillow, you've probably noticed that different emotions are recorded at different points on your body. Falling in love, for example, can register as an expansive, light and warm feeling in the chest. And a broken heart takes its name from the place where we feel it, in our hearts. Suddenly being moved by the emotion could make us "suffocate", or what we feel in our throats. A sudden disappointment or negative realization is recorded as a feeling of sinking into our guts. In fact, what distinguishes emotions from thoughts is that we typically feel them energetic even if they cough in the body. With a little introspection, we can easily see that our inner psychological life is mapped to specific points of the body, the chakras.

The chakras are arranged vertically, from the base of the spine you have to the crown of the head. From bottom to top are:

1. *Muladhara* or root chakra at the base of the spine
2. *Svadishthana* or sacral chakra, connected to the testicles or ovaries
3. *Manipura* or solar plexus chakra
4. *Anahata* or heart chakra , regardless of whether or not it is located in the heart, but close to it, in the center of the chest.
5. *Vishuddha* or throat chakra
6. *Ajña*, the so-called "third eye", located behind the forehead

7. *Sahasrara* or crown chakra , located at the top of the head

Each chakr a is represented by a lotus flower with a certain number of petals, which are also characterized by being the spokes of a wheel (*chakra*). These are actually minor channels that branch off from the chakras. The chakras are connected to various physical functions and levels of human psychological and spiritual development, the mind, emotions and higher levels of understanding. They are also connected with "seed syllables", or some mantric sounds in Sanskrit, different colors, eidade elements. Together they constitute a complete map of human existence, from our lowest functions to our highest potential.

Canals

AS I SAID BEFORE, THOUSANDS of *channels or nadis* (72,000, to be exact), which resemble veins or nerves, run through the subtle body. As for the seven main chakras, three channels are the most important: *shushumna, ida* and *pingala*. The *shushumna* is the central channel, while the ida and pingala are left and right respectively, although they are actually intertwined in and out of the chakras as a helical double strand of DNA, so that sometimes the left channel *is* on the right, and the right pingala channel is on the left. The chakras are the seven places where the three channels intersect as *a round trip and pingala* crossed in their winding course.

- *The unidirectional* is white. It is connected with the energy of the moon, the feminine principle, a refreshing quality and the Ganges River. In modern terms, it is also connected to the right hemisphere of the brain, which is commonly thought to be more intuitive, which governs the left half of the body. It ends in the left nostril.
- *Pingala*, red in color, is connected with solar energy, the masculine principle, a calorific effect and the Yamuna River. It is

connected to the left hemisphere of the brain, which is rational and associated with linear thinking and which governs the right half of the body. It ends in the right nostril.

- The *shushumna* runs directly from the root chakra to the crown, connecting the seven chakras. It has no color or attributes, but it is completely transparent, like empty space. It is also the course that the *kundalini* energy, which lies dormant or "rolled up" like a snake at the base of the spine, will embark on its journey from the root chakra to the crown when it wakes up, crossing each of the intermediate chakras in turn. But for most of us, it remains dormant.

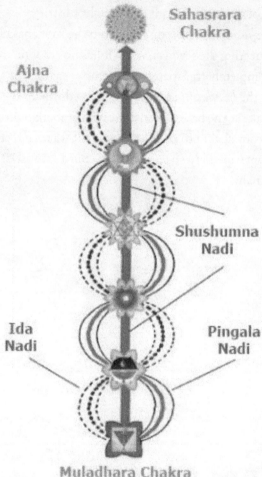

Ubicaciones Nadi

Sahasrara Chakra

Ajna Chakra

Shushumna Nadi

Ida Nadi

Pingala Nadi

Muladhara Chakra

NORMALLY, WE GO AND go back and *forth between round* trip and *ping her*, usually with an hour in each of them. If you compare it to your experience, you will notice that usually one of your nostrils is more open than the other, and this is the main nostril through which you breathe. For an hour, your breath will flow mainly through your left nostril, then the next hour through your right and so on. But there may also be an imbalance between the two. This will register as an imbalance in the masculine and feminine ways of your psyche, or in the processes of heating and cooling the body. It could manifest as anything from an illness to an emotional disorder.

Balance is restored through a series of practices. But one of the main goals is to awaken the latent energy of the kundalini by stimulating it through exercises designed to move the prana energy with the *round* trip and *pingala* in such a way that the kundalini rises through the central channel. If the energies enter the central channel in the correct way, they can lead to solid meditative stability and spiritual awakening. Your mind will become, like *shushumna*, transparent, peaceful and crystalline.

Therefore, in this system methods such as yoga and pranayama are employed to induce the energies to enter the central channel, where they will rise from the root chakra to the crown chakra, correcting any blockage or imbalance of chakras along the way. This is the main goal of working with the chakras.

The End of Spiritual Practice

PERHAPS IT WILL HELP at this point to say something about the ultimate spiritual goal of all this. From the point of view of this system, the ultimate reality of all things is an infinite, perfect and immaculate consciousness. You could call this ultimate consciousness God, or the Self, or the Absolute. Perhaps you would feel more comfortable calling it the Tao, or even the Universe.

Let's not cling to semantics here. What we are talking about is an absolute point of consciousness or immutable consciousness, a single immobile point that is the source of every differentiated experience. It is not dual, it does not know how to distinguish between the object and the subject, eternity and change, the creator and creation. So it doesn't matter what you call it. The point is to realize that *You are that*, in a sense You are already identical to your primordial state, Your true self beyond the blind, limited "I" of the ego.

All things find their unity in the absolute. This phenomenal world of plurality and variety that we experience with our senses is nothing more than an outpouring of divine energy games. Ultimate unity is never separated from pure consciousness.

In tantra, this ultimate being is called Shiva. Shiva is the last motionless, perfect and immutable point, the absolute consciousness untouched by the vicissitudes of the world. Shiva's energy or power arises as the infinite dance of the phenomenal world. This energy is called Shakti, and is considered the wife or consort of Shiva. But in reality, Shiva and Shakti, the staple of pure consciousness and the pulse and dynamism of life, are ultimately one.

Shiva is not a god "out there", but is just your pure consciousness beyond time and space. Similarly, Shakti is not an external goddess, but the energy and play of your experience. As individuals, we are not separated from the absolute, but are simply its various expressions, in the same way that the waves on the surface of the ocean are one with that same ocean.

In terms of the subtle body, Shakti is the kundalini energy that resides in the root chakra, while Shiva resides in the crown chakra. When Shakti breaks, he gets up to meet Shiva in the crown chakra and the two become one. This means that the dualistic back and forth of the energy moving in the ida and *pingala channels* ends, and its energies are unified in the no dual *shushumna* channel.

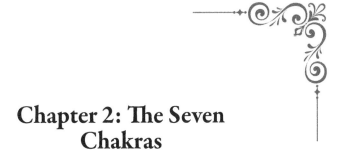

Chapter 2: The Seven Chakras

Now that we have a general idea of what the chakras are, what is their place within the total ecology of the subtle body, and how that subtle body relates to the goals of spiritual practice, we are ready to look at the chakras and their qualities one by one.

1. The Muladhara Chakra / Root Chakra

THE FIRST CHAKRA IS the *muladhara*, which means "base of the root", located at the base of the spine. The name itself provides the clue to its meaning. It refers to the basic physiological and psychological functions of the human organism, survival and instinct. As such, it has to do with activities related to security and survival, such as making money and getting food. *Muladhara* is the basis of the subtle body and the three main *nadis* of *ida*, *pingala* and *shushumna*. It is also the place where the latent kundalini is located .

The root chakra is visualized as a red lotus with four petals. As with ichakra, each of the "petals" (sometimes "rays") of the root chakra actually represents minor channels that branch off from it. So, in addition to the three main channels that run vertically through the body, the root chakra also has four minor channels that branch off from it, such as veins or nerves.

Its element is the earth. Since this chakra is the root or foundation of the subtle body system, it is connected with the energy of the earth. An imbalance in this chakra could include feelings of insecurity, especially in financial matters, food and shelter, which are directly related to physical survival. When the *muladhara* chakra is balanced, you feel safe, secure and well established in the solid quality of the earth.

This means that, in order to work in the higher chakras and more developed areas of life, you must first take care of your basic life situation. Do you have your life organized in terms of money and a place to live? Psychologically, do you feel safe and secure, or do you suffer from concern about survival-related areas such as finances, job security, etc.?

This part of your life forms the root or base of everything else, so if you don't take care of it sooner, the rest won't be solved. If your root chakra is weak, everything else, your sex life, social life, relationships, communication, intuition and spirituality, will be unstable. Everything will have collapsed because it does not rest on a secure base. So the lesson of the root chakra is: take care of your basic livelihood. Don't use spirituality or personal development as a way to avoid your responsibilities.

The color of *muladhara* is red and its element is, as it should be, the earth. The Earth, as an element in the five-element system, is defined by its solidity. It is the support for everything that lives in it. Similarly, the *muladhara* chakra is the support of the chakra system and our lives are built on its foundation. The seed syllable is *lam* (pronounced "lum"), which is the syllable of the earth element. Later in this book, when we talk about the practices for chakra activation, we will explain the meaning of seed syllables.

2. The Svadishthana Chakra / Sacral Chakra

THE *svadishthana* chakra (SWAH deesh TAH nuh), or sacral chakra, is the second chakra, located in the coccyx or genital region, near the root chakra and above it. The name *svadishthana* means "his dwelling place". It is related to the reproductive system and sexuality. Sexuality is very intimate, even private, hence the name, which suggests a very personal situation.

Because it is linked to sexuality, it is also linked to creativity and to the passionate energy of libido. The desire related to *svadishthana* can be mainly unconscious. Since we are dealing with sexuality and the raw emotional energy of libido, we are talking about a kind of wild, wild and difficult to control emotionality. It can also manifest as cruelty.

This is what the *vrittis* associated with its six petals or subsidiary channels suggests: affection, ruthlessness, destructiveness, delirium, contempt and paranoia. *Vritti are* like disturbances of consciousness. Here, as with other chakras, they correspond to the minor channels that branch off from this chakra and manifest themselves when energy moves through these channels.

The sacral chakra is represented by an orange lotus with six petals. His seed syllable is *vam*. Its element is water, an extravagant element that takes on multiple forms, can be frozen or liquid, can flow quickly and with great force ocon spa and delicacy, or gather in one place and remain still; it can erode surfaces or support life. The emotional quality of *svadishthana* is equally varied, with enormous creative and destructive potential.

Having worked in our basic life situation, we are ready to work on our emotional lives, starting from our passions and desires. The idea expressed by *svadishthana* is to balance the energy of our passions. Without training and without direction, this energy can slip under the surface of consciousness, bursting unexpectedly when it is somehow provoked. Working with *svadishthana*, we learn to harness this creative energy productively.

There are many reasons why the sacral chakra may be blocked or unbalanced. The trauma of sexual abuse is one of the reasons. Another may have to do with repressed desires. The destructive potential of passion is a threat to society, which seeks to control the way we express it. Each of us internalizes this social superstructure in our own mind, and then learns to push problematic feelings into unconsciousness.

So while none of the chakras are particularly *easy* to work with, working with *svadishthana* could be particularly volatile, as it can bring painful trauma and force us to face oppressive conditioning. But it is necessary to make the effort if we want to progress in our personal or spiritual growth. When this chakra is well balanced, we know how to pursue and express our desires, including sexual desires, in a positive way. We are not afraid of risks, but we are able to manage our emotional energy to face new challenges. We also get in touch with our innate creativity.

3. The Manipura Chakra / Solar Plexus Chakra

MANIPURA means "city of jewels". This is the solar plexus chakra, which is actually located slightly *above* the navel level. Its element is fire. Physically, it is connected to metabolism and the "fire" of digestion, which transforms food, extracting its nutrients and processing waste. Psychologically, it has to do with willpower, purpose, self-determination, fear and anxiety.

The solar plexus chakra is depicted as a ten-petaled yellow lotus. Its syllable is *ram*, the seed syllable of the fire element. Its function is transformative, fiery and useful.

In traditional Hindu medicine, digestion is compared to burning fire, which turns fuel into heat and light and leaves the ashes behind. Similarly, digestion transforms food, nourishing the body and contributing to its growth, giving it energy. It also leaves residues. The operation of one's personal free will in the world is also about transformation, shaping situations according to one's own will.

If *svadishthana* has to do with the energy of the power of libido and passion, especially as expressed with an intimate person, *manipura* is more interested in the exercise of willpower as a force of action in the public sphere of society. Here the emotional energy is more developed and civilized than in *svadishthana*. He found a mode of expression more suited to the social world, as opposed to the raw and unprocessed emotionality of the sacral chakra, which finds its usual home in private situations.

In the root chakra we have seen the basic survival instincts in action, in the sacral chakra the reproductive instinct. Here we see, for the first time, a more recognizable human quality, unlike what we have in common with animals. It is the emergence of a differentiated human consciousness that sees itself as an independent agent that goes ahead with its own agenda in the social sphere. So the key ideas around the *manipura chakra* include self-affirmation, trust, competence, effort, voluntad and purpose.

When it is unbalanced, it can physically manifest as poor digestion. Emotionally, an imbalance can arise in the form of excessive self-critical thoughts, shyness, fear, lack of confidence, what some call "paralysis of analysis". Or, on the other side of the imbalance, it can arise as a kind of stubborn stubbornness, as with people who are too sure of themselves and too strong of their will. By activating and balancing the solar plexus chakra, we can come to express our will safely and healthily without stepping on everyone else.

4. The Anahata Chakra / Heart Chakra

THE ANAHATA or "intact" chakra is commonly called the "heart chakra," but this is a bit misleading. Although *anahata* is located near the heart, it is actually in the center of the chest. There is a separate chakra, located slightly below and to the left of *anahata*, called *hrit*, literally "heart". But, since this has not been considered an important chakra in the system we are presenting, we will go ahead with the convention of calling the "heart" chakra *anahata*.

The name "intact" is curious, but it refers to the Vedic concept of intact sound. This is the primordial and uncreated sound of Om, which is the universal vibration of every human being. No one has ever made or "played" this sound, but it plays alone, so *anahata*. It is represented by a twelve-petaled lotus, green, with the yam of the seed syllable, which is the syllable of the air element.

As the name "intact" with *anahata* suggests, we are already moving beyond the realm of worldly thought and family activity for most of us, toward the rarefied atmosphere of the higher levels of being. *Anahata* is associated with feelings of love, not with the intimate erotic romance of lovers (which would be *svadishthana*), but with universal and impartial love. You could call it compassion or loving kindness.

Unlike personal love, which often seeks to manipulate the loved one, the love we are talking about does not care about protecting its own soil. It is quite altruistic. It does not have a center because it has no ego, so it is like the "intact sound" of Om, infiltrating everywhere of the same and impartial m anera.

We have seen the gradual development of animal levels of survival and sexuality, at the human level of willpower, which is selfish. *Anahata* is beginning to relate to a transpersonal and disinterested level, which most of us never reach. So we can say that the heart chakra is the beginning of true spirituality.

An imbalance in the heart chakra can physically lead to respiratory disorders, heart disease, chest pain, and immune system disorders. Emotionally, it can manifest as fear of being alone, bitterness, lack of emotional availability, coldness, selfishness. Or we may be suffocated in our love, trying to control our killers. These are manifestations of neurosis at the level of the heart chakra.

When the heart chakra is balanced, we become generous, open, caring, and sensitive to the needs and feelings of others in a positive, non-neurotic way. The language we use is a clear indication: let's say someone has a "big heart," or let's talk about "opening the heart." This refers to the qualities of someone who has a well-balanced heart chakra.

5. The Vishuddha Chakra / Throat Chakra

THE NAME OF THIS CHAKRA, *vishuddha* or *vishuddhi*, means "very pure". It is located in the throat region. It has to do with the power of the word, understood here in a broad sense as the ability to communicate by any linguistic or symbolic medium. This includes not only speaking and writing, but also the arts, which are symbolic forms of personal expression.

The first three chakras were related to survival, sexuality and willpower. The fourth chakra, in the heart, has introduced a new way of being that is not based on the manipulations of the ego, but is decentralized, impartial and affectionate. Having developed that sense of love within us, we find that he desires to find expression. He needs a way to communicate to himself.

The throat chakra is represented by a blue lotus with sixteen petals. The sixteen petals correspond to the sixteen vowels of classical Sanskrit phonology. The element connected with the throat chakra is space, and the seed syllable of this chakra is the syllable of the space element, ham. The word for space in Sanskrit can also mean sky, so that's why this chakra is blue.

Normally, when we talk, we do it a little recklessly. Sometimes we use the word in a manipulative way to deceive others or to sow discord. Or we use our words as weapons, to abuse and do harm. We can speak to ourselves udadamente, without considering the impact that our words can have on others. Therefore, vicious voices can begin, simply because we wanted to entertain ourselves with the conversation.

Vishuddha, the "very pure" chakra, forces us to maintain purity in the way we communicate. The way we do this is suggested by the elementary nature of the chakra itself: we introduce space. Instead of letting the words come to light in a reckless hurry, we pronounce them carefully. Let there be a space between words and phrases, and rest in that space just a moment before continuing. In this way, we bring a meditative presence to our discourse.

This way of speaking reflects the process of meditation on breathing. First there is an exhalation, which is like a speech in itself. The breath comes out and dissolves in space. So, let's breathe. We are not in a hurry to suck our breath into our lungs to keep talking. Inhalation should be relaxedand comfortable, an opportunity to rest. Only then do we continue to speak.

An imbalance in this chakra can manifest as an inability to express oneself verbally. The inability to express oneself can be very distressing; it makes you feel helpless and voiceless. You have no way to make yourself heard. Alternatively, you can abuse the word in the way described above. In both cases it reflects that something is wrong with the throat chakra.

When *vishuddha* is balanced, your speech comes naturally and easily. It has an easy to scroll quality, pleasant and persuasive. Speak true, kind, and timely words that are beneficial to others. If you are an artist, your art becomes an expression of your worthy mind, and communicates a healthy and kind perspective.

6. The Ajña Chakra / The Third Eye Chakra

THE SIXTH CHAKRA CALLED *ajña*, is located superficially in the center of the forehead, between the eyebrows and above them. Internally, it is located in the pineal gland. It is often called the "third eye" because of its relationship to seeing, not physical sight, but understanding intuition. So we are talking about a special kind of knowledge. Sanskrit *ajña* means "to command", as in the command of the master or guru. *Ajña* is the command center of the chakra system. Media between the upper self of the crown chakra and the rest of the underlying chakras.

But it is also related to the word knowledge, especially of spiritual voipo. We are still talking about a differentiated type of knowledge, not the highest knowledge of the absolute. This chakra is also connected to the faculties of imagination and sleep.

Ajña is represented by a two-petaled lotus of a deep indigo color. *Ida* and *pingala* end here. Their duality does not reach a higher level than this. It is associated with the mental element and its seed syllable is *Om*, the primordial sound. Its presiding deity is Ardhanarishvara, a hermaphrodite form of Shiva-Shakti together. The union of male and female in a deity suggests that we are now approaching non-duality.

When we reach the level of the third eye, we have made contact with a sense of universal love and purified our course. Now we need to develop a sense of wisdom. Without wisdom, our hearts can be expansive and loving, our speech may be pure in its intent, but we will behave stupidly out of ignorance. We still have the opportunity to ruin things.

Understanding the third eye is not just a kind of psychic ability, although it is something that is traditionally included here as well. *Ajña* has to deal with a penetrating vision that sees things completely and precisely. This understanding is so sharp, so ruthless, that it penetrates through every illusion.

When the third eye chakra is unbalanced, it can lead to daydreaming, getting lost in a fantasy world, and even illusions and hallucinations. It is as if the calibration of the sensor is turned off. Or we may find ourselves rigidly attached to a belief system, religion or ideology. Our thoughts and concepts become solid and inflexible.

When *ajña* is balanced and fully operational, the mind becomes extremely clear, perceptive, penetrating and intuitive. It has a laser beam focus that hits the point with precision. He sees easily through deception and manipulation, including the ego's changing self-deceptions, and very easily perceives the truth of things.

7. The Sahasrara Chakra / Crown Chakra

THE *sahasrara chakra* or "thousand petals" is called the crown chakra, and is the apex of the chakra system. It is said to be located on the crown of the head, or in the space above it, depending on the tradition that is consulted.

As the name suggests, this chakra is represented by a lotus with a thousand petals. Petals are of many colors. The crown chakra is the last white light, which refracts, as through a prism, in every color of the visible spectrum. There is no element connected to this chakra, nor a seed syllable. Instead, it is associated with the pure consciousness we mentioned earlier, the Absolute, which is identical, or the higher Self. If it has an "element", it is that of emptiness or final emptying, the last unit beyond all attributes and qualities.

Sahasrara is both the source of every manifestation and the destiny of the spiritual struggle. This chakra is the point of arrival of the kundalini energy at the end of its journey. It is the residence of Shiva. When kundalini *reaches sahasrara,* Shiva and Shakti, male and female, are united in the latter non-dual state. At this point, one does not reach *either rvikalpasamadhi,* which is the complete identification of oneself with the Absolute. This is enlightenment or awakening.

This chakra is inconceivable. It cannot be understood from an ordinary, dualistic point of view. Everything we say about it is purametafora, word and image, a finger pointing to the moon, but not the moon itself. *Sahasrara* is the supreme light of pure consciousness and not dual.

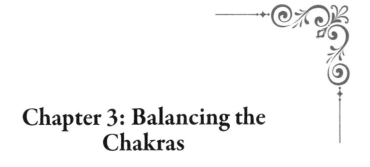

Chapter 3: Balancing the Chakras

I'm sure you've probably heard of balancing the chakras and abrir the chakras. Well, what do these phrases really mean? Given the dangers involved, it is good that we are a little attentive to the idea.

One important thing to note is that chakra balancing and chakra opening are two distinct things. At first, it is not a good idea to try to open the chakras. Such a careless approach will leave you vulnerable to unscrupulous people and negative energies.

Of course, the ultimate goal of italian awakening is to open the chakras and let the kundalini energy flow unhindered. But this can only happen once you have strengthened your system. You must first give him a little more strength, rewire everything, because at this time he can not stand that level of tension. Such an accident would do nothing but fry your circuits, perhaps permanently.

Close the Chakras?

SO IT IS VERY IMPORTANT to balance the chakras. It sounds a bit strange, but that could mean *closing* some chakras that are open, or at least closing them partially.

As I mentioned, there are bad people out there who will feed on your energy if you become very vulnerable. They will only suck you until you dry. These people are called "energy vampires."

In addition, there is a lot of pollution in our energy environment. We receive the information we consume as much as the food we eat. And the air we breathe is a vector for polluted energy to enter our system. Because we absorb prana by breathing, pollution in the air can also contaminate our subtle body if it is too open to such influences.

Think of each chakra as if it were a home. If you leave the doors and windows open, thieves, murderers and wildlife can come in and do whatever they want. On the other hand, if you take off the security of the doors, close the windows and close yourself like Boo Radley in *To Kill a Mockingbird*, then you isolate yourself from the world. Then you become a prisoner of your boredom, hardly a better way to do things.

The balanced approach is to use your best judgment on which guests to invite into your home and which intruders to reject.

Identify and work on imbalances

BEFORE YOU TRY TO BALANCE your cha kras, you must first recognize where the imbalances occur. All that theory we've looked at before is useful here.

Look at your life: which areas are shaky or struggling? See Chapter 2 for help if you need it. That chapter is meant to give you a good idea of how the chakra system maps into different areas of life. Explain what can happen when each chakra is unbalanced. I will also cover chakra imbalances in this chapter, as well as what you can do about it.

For example, if you feel uncomfortable expressing your feelings in a relationship, your heart chakra may be too limited. To restore balance, we recommend that you do practices to open that chakra specifically.

Or maybe you find yourself *being very* dedicated and *very* selfless. You may not consider your needs. In that case, finding balance can mean closing the heart chakra a bit, while working on strengthening other chakras that could put you in a weak position, perhaps strengthening your willpower by working on the solar plexus chakra or your self-expression with the throat chakra.

Therefore, the first step is to identify where imbalances may occur. This will require some introspection and reflection, and perhaps some trial and error. All right. It's a process. It takes time.

So, once you know the imbalance, you'll be able to address specific areas of improvement. There is no one-size-fits-all solution. You just need to get to know yourself a little, do some reflection and then start working on it, which is a learning process in itself.

In what follows, I will explain a little about what you can do to balance each chakra. I have given more weight to the practical steps you can take to change the way you lead your life. This is because you can always find a lot of training elsewhere on different healing techniques with types of crystals and herbs, various meditations and so on that should balance your chakras.

These methods have a merit, but if you trust only them, then you run the risk of dedicating yourself to the navel-solipsistic, and then ask yourself where the practical benefit is. The practical advantage comes from the adoption of practical measures. There is no shortcut to this. Other healing techniques are helpful, but their role is to integrate and support the concrete changes you make in your life. Someone with balanced chakras needs to be effective and skillful in the way they live their lives, so that's what I chose to emphasize here.

1. Balancing Muledhara, the root chakra

Signs of imbalance in the root chakra can be a failure of survival instincts, a failure to take care of basic needs related to food, shelter and finances. It can also include addiction and loss of interest in dealing with life's challenges. If you find that, when adversity comes, you don't have much struggle in you, you probably need to work in *the muladhara*.

Alternatively, if you're *very* survival-oriented, you could live in a bunker or off-grid in a cabin in the woods with lots of gold bars hidden under the floorboards. But you are likely to have another problem, because for most of us our modern life protects us from immediate danger, which stuns our animal instincts.

There are a few techniques you can use to balance muladhara, ranging from obviously practical to less obvious. Here are some things you can do:

- Go *camping*. Go out into the desert alone. Take only what you need to shelter, cook and defend yourself. It is even better if the place is remote enough and there is some danger involved. Because? Because nothing sets in motion a weak survival instinct like reminding yourself that you are an animal, and the name of the game is survival of the most suitable.

- In this line, you can also **do a death-defying sport** such as skydiving or *bungee jumping*. Details are not important. Just make sure it's exciting and risky. Again, the idea is to put your survival instinct into action. But don't sue me if everything goes wrong and you end up in a hospital bed or 6 feet underground, because that's *inherently risky*. You will only have to take responsibility for what is happening, good or bad.

- Keep a journal and take some time to **write down what will happen if you let your worst habits get out of control**. I think you probably already have a good idea of where your weaknesses lie, so be honest with yourself. Brutally honest. Imagine if you freely indulged in your laziness, inertia, naivety and irresponsibility. What would happen?
  To write. Fear it. (Fear is not your enemy. It is an indicator that there is danger, so learn to respect it.) So, you decide not to let this happen. Take all necessary measures to cultivate pro-survival habits.

- **Be more physical**. Do something physical, sports, exercise, dance, to get in touch with your body. Boxing and martial arts are also great, because they are physical, they tune your senses and instincts, and you could get hurt. Lord, do not shake your head. This also applies to you. Risky activity is not just for children.

- **Do yoga**. Later in this book I will give a brief index of the yoga poses useful for balancing each of the seven chakras. But for now, suffice it to say that yoga is an amazing way to balance all the chakras in general. In addition, it is physical, so it also counts as an example of the previous method.
- Meditate on the **color red**. Visualize it, especially at the base of the spine, at the root chakra. Use more red. Wear jewelry with red precious stones, such as ilrubino. This is the color of the root chakra, so focusing on it will help you tune in to that frequency.
- **Consume more root vegetables**. Potatoes, onions, carrots, radishes, beets and so on. Beetroot is also red in color. The earthly quality of these foods resonates with the root chakra.

2. Balancing Svadishthana, the Sacral Chakra

Signs of *svadishthana imbalance* include sexual frustration, inability to get carried away when having sex, and loss of interest in sex. More generally, loss of creativity and inspiration. Physically this can manifest as various sexual dysfunctions, such as impotence.

You may also be overly energetic: an excess of sexual appetite and even sex addiction are signs that you may need to reduce it.

Here are some things you can do:

- **Make yourself more attractive**. One of the reasons why you may be sexually frustrated or lose interest in sex is because others don't find you attractive. If you were targeting this and getting more attention from potential sexual partners or your current partner, chances are your interest in sex will also increase.

  Now, it's easier said than done. How to attract sexual interest is far beyond the scope of this book. But it is not that there was a shortage of literature and advice on this. However, some tips: get in shape. Wear attractive clothes. Be confident and bold, even if you have to pretend.

- If you're having the opposite problem and your sexual appetite is too high, keep **higher standards**. I'm not saying you should be a prudent, but maybe it's not a good idea to be too airy about sex. This is a serious matter with potentially serious consequences, and it should be treated in this way.

  When you sleep with someone, you get entangled with them even on an energetic level. This affects you mentally and emotionally. Therefore, be a little cautious and choose onlyworthy pairs that have healthy minds and treat you respectfully.

- Learn to feel more comfortable expressing your sexuality through **dance**. The dance is very physical and sensual, so it is a good way to tune into the sacral chakra. Esto will also open you up to more creative energies. Men who are skeptical about this simply consider dance to be very *sexy*, and anyone who may be interested in you sexually will probably find you more attractive just because you can bail it out well.

- **Eliminate the habit of porn**. The jury does not yet know whether pornography increases sexual appetite or decreases motivation to enter into intimacy with real-life humans, but in any case, it is not the ideal way to activate the sacral chakra. Working with the chakras should be to reduce the illusion and be more in tune with your inner and outer reality. Looking at the images on the screen is the opposite of this and only tricks your brain into thinking that there are sexual opportunities present.

- If you're in a relationship, **keep the romance alive**. Go out on romantic dates. Prepare dinner for your partner and eat it by candlelight. Treat yourself to a luxurious full body massage. Let them give you a massage. Tell him what you love about his body. Step into the hot tub together or take a bubble bath. Don't have a bathtub? Find a place to bathe naked at night.

Don't let routine and boredom kill passion. Especially if the relationship is not new, you have to work to keep it alive. So, sometimes, try to behave young, stupid and in love.

- Again, **yoga** puts you in touch with your body. And it induces a healthy and balanced flow of energy in the subtle body, which balances the chakras and promotes healthy sexual function and expression. It will also improve your physical and mental fitness, which will make you more attractive to other people.

- **Visualize orange**, especially in the area of your sacral chakra. Wear orange clothing and orange gemstones such as carnelian and citrine. Psychologically, it will tune your mind to the sacral chakra that resonates with its color.

- **Eat sweet, sticky, juicy and tropical fruits**. There is something inherently sensual about mangoes and pomegranates (compared, for example, to turnips or beans) that can awaken libido.

3. Balance manipura, the chakra of the solar plexus

Signs of imbalance can be shyness or fear, low self-esteem, fear of rejection, hypersensitivity to perceived criticism and insults, poor concentration, passivity and self-criticism. Physically, the imbalance can also manifest as digestion problems.

An excess of energy in this chakra can take the form of excessive confidence, anger, stubbornness, an excessively demanding personality, behaving excessively aggressively, being ambitious to the point of ignoring the risks and consequences of his actions for others. In other words, the stubborn selfishness that goes on blindly. It can also manifest itself as overly critical and critical of others.

Here are some things you can do:

- If *the manipura* is not very active, try playing **competitive games and sports**. Learning to push your edge against other players in a competitive arena can do wonders for learning the fundamental lesson of this chakra: the ability to assert your personal will in life.
- If *the manipura* is overactive, on the other hand, you may try **cooperative activities**. This is also part of being a good member of a team. If you think of life as a complex system of nested games, then one of the most important metagames is to play fairly. What is the goal of the metagame? Play in such a way that other players will want to play with you in the future.

   This is fundamentally being a good player, or a nice, fair and friendly person. It does not mean being faint of heart or weak of weakness. There's a healthy balance to be found in life, and if you're always crushing other people, they won't want to deal with you in the future. This is your loss, not theirs.

- For a hyperactive solar plexus chakra, try to let **the other person get away with it** sometimes. Not all battles have to be won. Sometimes it gives in. And try not to be a badperdedor for it. People in your life will appreciate you for knowing how to choose your battles. And if you sacrifice some of your desires for theirs, you'll be amazed at how often they'll be happy to reciprocate by doing things you enjoy.

- If you have the opposite problem and act like a doormat, sometimes **defend yourself**. Now, it's easier said than done. Maybe you should start small. Stick to issues where the stakes are low.

   Maybe you're not ready to break into your boss's office and ask for a raise. So choose an easier goal: "I don't really want to eat Chinese food tonight. We order pizza instead." You don't have to declare war, but at least you can express your wishes and push a little to get them. This is a good start!

- If you have the root and sacral chakras in order, then you have a good base for working on *manipura*. So make sure you don't have any more basic problems to work on in the first place. Once you understand this, you will be in a better position to assert your will.

- Don't forget that some **yoga poses** can help here, as we'll cover in a later section. If you want to understand the benefits here, consider how you support yourself when you feel fearful, passive, or unstable. Your posture probably isn't very good and chances are your head won't be held up very high. Most people drop their shoulders and shrink.

  Now consider your posture when you feel relaxed, confident and firm. Your back is probably straight, your shoulders square, and you're easily able to make eye contact with other people.

  This posture communicates confidence and strength of voluntad. It makes you look like an effective person. And, due to a kind of feedback loop that happens between our body and our mind, *you will feel* more confident and effective just by staying that way.

- Meditate **on the yellow color** in the solar plexus chakra. Wear bright yellow clothes. Wear gold jewelry or yellow gemstones such as yellow or amber topaz.

- Foods that stimulate balance in *manipura* include various cereals: wheat, flax, rice, and so on. Bread and pasta resonate with this chakra. Also try adding ginger and turmeric to your meal. They promote healthy digestion and healthy functioning of the solar plexus chakra .

4. Balancing Anahata, the heart chakra

Imbalance in the heart chakra can manifest as the inability to express emotions to others, especially feelings of love and appreciation, but also the lack of expression of disappointment, sadness and hurt feelings. You don't need to put your heart in your hand, but it's nice if you can share the feelings of your heart with the people who are closest to you.

Physical symptoms can include irregular heart rate and arrhythmia, chest pains, even a heart attack. Of course, if you experience any of these symptoms, they are very serious. So you should definitely see a doctor for them, and only after that work on chakra balancing.

An overactive heart chakra takes the form of excessive stormy emotions, excessive sadness, pain, despair, feelings of betrayal and pain, anger, emotional need, etc. If such emotions run through you uncontrollably, making you feel like a ship at sea, beaten and thrown by stormy vitos, then you need to work on the heart chakra.

Anger in the case of an overactive heart chakra is different from a hyperactive solar plexus chakra. If *the manipura* is overactive, anger is the emotional reaction when faced with frustration or resistance. If *anahata* is overactive, anger is just an emotion in a chaotic stream.

There are many things you can do for an imbalance in the heart chakra:

- If you think your heart chakra is inactive, thenat this time **you pick up the phone and call someone you love**. It could be your mother or father, another relative, a loved one, or a friend. Never mind. Choose someone with whom you never communicate emotionally, but to whom you care in your dog party. Tell them what they mean to you and how much you appreciate them.

  You don't have to use the word with "A" if you prefer not to. It's not so much the words you use as the meaning: that you care about that person, that you care about them, and that you appreciate what they bring into your life.

- If, on the other hand, your life is characterized by emotional turmoil, we recommend that you take a step back and take a look at the cause.

  Do not come to the conclusion that the problem is with you. It could be that you have allowed someone to enter your heart who is not very kind to you. Does your emotional chaos come from someone else's drama and manipulations? If so, take whatever action you need to take to **distance yourself from the person who is causing you distress in** a clean, gentle way, without hurting or blaming them, but also with a firm determination and confidence that you must first take your well-being and movement.

- If the source does not depend on someone else, then a solution is more difficult. It could be that your emotions are turbulent because of the anxieties and fears that come with past traumas.

  It is worth keeping this in mind, but you do not have to keep reviewing painful episodes from the past. Mindfulness **meditation** is a good way to distance yourself from your emotions.

  The point of care is not to perform an emotional amputation. The point is to get in touch with the background, the space in which emotions are produced. The energy of emotions is very vivid and raw, but it occurs in an immutable space of naked consciousness. It remains in consciousness rather than in the constant movement of emotional energy. When you learn to rest in that inherent opening, the emotional turbulence will subside on its own.

- To this end, you may want **to participate in a meditation course.** Zen meditation is a great option for people who suffer from excessive emotions and thoughts, because it is very disciplined and does not offer space for distractions and entertainment. If you can find a local Zen center where you can get meditation instruction and stay *zazen*, you will be making great strides to promote a greater sense of inner peace and emotional tranquility.

Intuitive meditation or *vipassana* is also another very powerful form of meditation to cultivate a calm, precise and spacious mind. There is also a lot of scientific research on insightful meditation and other types of careful meditation that proves its effectiveness in treating depression and anxiety.

- Again, **yoga** is very good at promoting emotional balance. You'll know if you've ever had a really good and healing yoga session. You just *feel* better physically and emotionally. For the heart chakra as for all chakras, there are specific poses you can do to direct it to balance and healing.

- Meditate on the **green color**, especially the light green in the center of your pecho. Wear green clothes or green jewelry, such as emeralds, jade or green quartz.

- Surround yourself with greenery when **visiting the park or a botanical garden** or hiking. The human mind loves plants and feels happier and more comfortable among trees, grass and flowers.

- **Do some gardening** or keep the plants in pots and take care of them. Apart from the previous point about vegetation, gardening helps you get in touch with the attentive side of yourself, because you have to take responsibility for the growth and health of another living being. It's a good way to develop your nutrient side without having to raise a baby or clean up your excrement.

- Eat **green leafy vegetables**, spinach, cabbage, broccoli, etc. Herbal teas, especially tulsi, also heal the heart chakra.

5. Balance Vishuddha, the throat chakra

The four lower chakras are connected to the vital and worldly needs that people have, which are built on top of each other: survival, reproduction, vo luntad and love. Love is the link between the higher and lower priorities of human life. It is the pivot between the worldly and spiritual planes of our existence. You must take care of these priorities before you can work on spiritual levels .

The imbalance in *vishuddha* can take the form of impossibility or inability to express oneself, poor verbal communication, inarticulate speech. If what you say is constantly misunderstood by others, it could be because you're not saying it well. This is the sign of an underdeveloped throat chakra.

Other signs of imbalance include frequent lies, dissimulation, or any dishonest speech. Insincere speech, gossip and nonsensical gossip can also indicate a hyperactive throat chakra. Maybe you are too energetic in the way you express your opinions, others find you stubborn and want you to stay quiet sometimes.

Physically, the feeling of a "lump in the throat" is a symptom that this chakra is receiving more energy than it can bear. Constant problems associated with throat, sore throat, laryngitis, tonsillitis, etc. They may be related to an imbalance in *vishuddha*.

Here's what you can do:

- **Keep a journal or journal**. Just write more. Writing is also a form of self-expression, and if you can learn to write more articulately, you can also learn to speak more articulately.
- **Learn another language**. It's hard to do, but it definitely boosts your verbal skills. It also expands your mind: language influences the way we think, and if we speak a different language, we will also come to think differently. Or at least we will expand the scope of our thinking. It's a great mental challenge.
- The throat chakra is not only connected to verbal speech, but

also to literary arts, singing and music. Any kind of **learning** will develop this chakra. **Taking lessons from a musical instrument** or singing lessons will also balance an inactive throat chakra. Even if you only sing in the shower, that's fine. Sing with all your heart. Don't be shy.

- **Pay attention to what sdice** s. Learn to practice mindfulness in speech. If you pay attention to how you feel emotionally and physically when you speak, you will quickly find that there is a big difference between honest and dishonest speech. If you speak shonesta or insincere and too negligent, you will have a bad feeling. It will also be recorded physiologically.

  If you say true words that are useful to others and meaningful, they will strengthen you emotionally and physically. You will become a more reliable and respected person. People will listen to you, listen to your advice and give importance to your words. You will have a gravity that cannot be ignored.

- Visualize a blue healing light in your throat. Wear sky blue clothes. Observe the bright blue sky on a cloudless day and let your sense of awareness expand with it. Use blue gemstones, such as sapphire or turquoise.

- Drinking more water, juices and other fluids helps the healing and balance of this chakra. Acidic fruits such as lemon and kiwi also help. Increased salt consumption also benefits the throat chakra.

6. Balancing Ajña, the third eye chakra

Signs of imbalance in *ajña* could be an underdeveloped side, especially if nothing else. It may include a lack of imagination or excessive cynicism and skepticism about spirituality (a moderate amount of skepticism is healthy). You may also lack common sense, intelligence, or a keen intuition about things.

Hyperactivity in *ajña* could result in the loss of dreams and fantasies. Or it could mean a completely unrealistic and fantastic "spirituality", which is disconnected from the concrete realities of everyday life. You might imagine seeing all kinds of visions in meditation, for example, when you are really deceiving yourself.

Physical symptoms can include headaches and various brain problems.

Here's what you can do:

- If the third eye chakra is inactive, try **to remember your dreams**. Write them down when you wake up for the first time in the morning. Consider its meaning.
- If it helps you, learn more about dream interpretation, such as **Jungian deep psychology**. There is a deeper symbolic meaning in dreams and myths, and learning to speak this language will not only give you a deeper appreciation of the spiritual side of life, but will also allow you to consult the guidance of your inner self by understanding the language of symbols it speaks.
- **Pay attention to coincidences**. Matches can be significant. Significant coincidences are called *synchronicities*. Don't overdo it with this, or you could end up in a fantasy world with your imagination. Don't take 100% synchronicities seriously. Instead, take it seriously somewhere in the 50-90% range and only look at it as a guide if they resonate with you at a deep level of truth.
- If you have the opposite problem and are drifting into a false and unreal fantasy "spirituality," then it is probably because you are using spirituality to escape more concrete problems in your worldly existence. Then **work on your lower chakras**. There is something you are avoiding. Pay attention to this.
- **Do not be led astray by drugs**, especially drugs that have a dreamlike effect. You know which ones I'm talking about. Whatever you like, enjoy it in moderation.

- I receive an **indigo-colored light in** the center of the forehead. Imagine it healing yourself and instilling in you a divine vision and a sharper, more penetrating perception.

7. *Balancing the Sahasrara, the crown chakra*

Almost no one has balanced this chakra as it is closed to almost everyone. *Sahasrara* is a secret that it hides from itself. This is your direct link with the Divine, with the absolute source of being as such. Occasionally it can open spontaneously in a moment of ecstasy and spiritual revelation. But having the doors open all the time would be intolerable for most people, unless the other six chakras were very well balanced and healthy, with a balanced flow of energy between them.

If you have no sense of connection with the divine, with the purpose of your life, no sense of meaning or ultimate identity, this suggests that your connection with this chakra is completely disconnected.

Here are some first steps you can take to do a conoxion with your higher self:

- One way to connect with this chakra is to do more spiritual activities **such as meditation and prayer.** Here the goal of meditation is a little different. It's not about finding balance or emotional peace. It is about slowly undoing the games of the ego. *Sahasrara transcends* the ego and the identity of the limited and worldly ego. You are yielding the limited, worldly ego to a higher plane of being. So activating this chakra is the end of the game of spiritual practice. It's not something you can hope to achieve right now, but you can start working to achieve it.
- If you feel adrift, meaningless, and want to connect with your higher sense of purpose, then read the **life of the great spirit masters** . Contemplate their example: the selfless and heroic way in which they lived their lives with tenderness and

compassion, how they treated others, how they behaved. This will give you an idea of what human life is when it is lived at its highest level of purpose.

- The **white color** contains all the colors of the visible spectrum, suggesting at the same time a purity, untouched by the dirt of the world. Meditate on a bright white light on your crown, which refracts in a rainbow prism of a thousand colorsand at the edges. Imagine that this light fills you with a higher sense of purpose beyond your personal concerns and connects you to a divine consciousness.

- Wear more linen. Use white or transparent precious stones such as transparent diamonds or quartz .

Chapter 4: Working with the Chakras

At this point, you're probably getting an idea of the extent of the problem. The subtle body and the yogic systems that operate in it are extremely complex issues. As I said before, although the seven chakra system is the most popular in modern times, there are also many other systems. There are also many practice systems for the chakras, both ancient and modern.

The fact is that there is no quick and magical way to open the chakras. And if there was, it would be extremely inadvisable for a beginner to try such a thing. The chakras of people without training are not very functional. Mostly they remain inactive, although they can stir from time to time. Suddenlymake the doors of its operation shine would cause all kinds of danger.

Unfortunately, people who open their chakras prematurely, accidentally or on purpose, may end up interned in institutions. They may suffer from hallucinations, dissociation, delusions, paranoia, etc. It is much better to go with a gradual cleaning program and balance them in preparation for a day to open them, if you ever choose it. The previous chapter gave you some practical tips on how to do it.

However, I would like to give you an overview of what such a path would look like. This is an aerial view, a broad scheme, which aims only to give a general idea of the shape of things. We will also review some initial practices to start getting in touch with the energies of the chakras and give them some fine tuning. These practices are intended as entry points for beginners. If you find that this path makes you feel good, you should find a teacher and find more advanced literature on the subject.

Kundalini

WE HAVE ALREADY TALKED a little bit about kundalini, and how it relates to the whole system of the subtle body and the goal of yogic practice. Covering kundalini correctly would require at least one more book, but we'll say a few more words about it here.

A kundalini awakening refers to the excitement of latent energy lying coiled in the *muladhara* chakra at the base of the spine. There are two ways in which this energy can be released: intentionally, as a result of practices aimed at awakening and elevating it, and involuntarily, in sensitive individuals who respond to some trigger.

While spontaneous kundalini rashes are known to occur prematurely and unintentionally, they are somewhat unusual and downright undesirable. When this happens, the suddenly awakened energy of the kundalini can explode upwards very strongly. I have already mentioned some of the possible effects of premature chakra opening.

Hatha yoga

THE PHYSICAL BODY IS purified and trained through the practice of hatha yoga, which is more or less the type of dynamic and physical yoga now famous all over the world. It implies the union of body movement and editative concentration. This prepares the body to sit for long periods of time in order to practice pranayama or breath control. But the various positions or asanas of hatha yoga alone help to purify the chakras and balance them. Below is a list of useful asanas for chakra work:

1. *Muladhara*: siddhasana, tadasana, tiryakatadasana, marjari asana

2. *Svadishthana*: siddhasana, ustrasana, padahastasana, bhujangasana, paschimottasana
3. *Manipura*: advasana, makarasana, tiryakatadasana, ashtanganamaskara, bhujangasana, dhanurasana, setu asana, halasana
4. *Anahata*: bhujangasana, dhanurasana
5. *Vishudda*: ustrasana, up to utthanasana, parvatasana, bhujangasana, dhanurasana, halasana
6. *Ajña*: shavasana, advasana, tadasana, ashvasanchalanasana, bhujangasana

Finally, the classic position for sitting meditation, the lotus or padmasana position, calms the subtle energies and directs their flow upwards from the root chakra to the crown chakra.

All these asanas can be found in my other book, *The Yoga Beginner's Bible*.

Pranayama

PRANAYAMA is often translated as "breath control". Here the word *prana* does not mean breathing, but the subtle energy that is connected with the breath. Pranayama works directly with this energy by manipulating the breath through a series of different exercises involving inhalation, exhalation, and internal and external re-ention of the breath. These affect the flow of prana through the channels of the subtle body.

There are many pranayama practices, but one of the simplest to promote chakra health is called *anulomaviloma pranayam* a, or alternative breathing of the nose. It is relatively safe for beginners to practice:

- Start by sitting cross-legged, with your back straight. The lotus position (*padmasana*) and the posture of the masters (*siddhasana*) are idealpositions , but if they are too tiring for you, sit in the most comfortable position of *sukhasana*. All these positions are explained in my other book, The Yoga Beginner's Bible.

- Rest your left hand on your knee.
- Bend the index finger and the middle of the right hand. The thumb, ring finger and little finger should be extended.
- Close your eyes and breathe slowly and gently for ten breaths. Relax and keep an eye on your breathing.
- Gently press your right thumb against your right nose to close it. Inhale slowly through the left nostril. Inhale completely, with all the diaphragm and chest.
- Now release the right nostril and close the left nostril with the ring finger. Exhale slowly through right lanarice, completely expelling all the air from the lungs.
- Without moving your fingers, keep your left nostril closed and breathe through your right nostril.
- Again close the right nostril with your right thumb and slowly exhale through your left nostril, emptying your lungs.
- This completes a round. Take seven laps a day, preferably the first thing in the morning when your mind is free of thoughts, or at night right after the sun. Do not practice alternating breathing from the nostrils directly during sunrise or sunset.
- After completing seven rounds, rest your right hand on your knee and simply relax your attention. Let the breath go up and down naturally, without conscious interference. Rest in the open field of consciousness without letting yourself be distracted by the train of thoughts or focusing on something in particular.

There are more advanced forms of alternative breathing in the nose that involve regulating the relationship between the duration of inhalation and exhalation, but to begin with, this simple version is a great way to calm the energy in the body. Alternative breathing balances the flow of energy in the left and right channels, *ida* and *pingala*. This produces a feeling of balance, centrality and peace of mind. It purifies the two channels and stimulates good health by inducing the flow of energy to the body's organs. By balancing the left or right channels, you stimulate the flow of energy into the central channel, which heals the chakras and makes them balance.

There are many other pranayama practices, such as fire breathing (agniprasana), but they are beyond the scope of this book. Pranayam a traditionally comes after a period of body training through yoga poses and should be practiced together with asanas. Like all the practices mentioned in this book, it is best to do it under the direction of a qualified and experienced teacher, who can give you personal instructions and adapt the methods according to your particular needs.

Before we get into a description of the next exercise, let's talk a little about the notion of samskara. *Samskara* can be treated as training or conditioning. All the negative experiences of the past, from minor to major traumas, create negative samskara in the body-mind. They can make us feel more vulnerable or defensive. They condition our reactions to certain stimuli. These samskaras are left as impressions in the chakras and modify the energy of that chakra in an unhealthy way.

As an extreme example, a soldier returning from war with PTSD (*post-traumatic stress* disorder) might have very strong samskara imprinted on the root and heart chakras. These samskaras could take the form of a persistent sense of danger stored in the root chakra, which sometimes explodes in an episode where you feel particularly insecure. Or it could be a shutdown of the energy of the heart chakra , as a result of guilt for extreme violence in time of war.

Before any truly spiritual work can begin, it is necessary to work on these samskaras by gently healing and balancing the chakras. If you try to jump into a more advanced practice too early, a sudden awakening of the kundalini energy could explode through the chakras, triggering all these impressions at once and triggering a psychotic flare-up. Therefore, the first steps should be to establish a secure foundation by leading a healthy lifestyle, training the body through yoga and quilting its energies through the most delicate practices of pranayama. We can also start working on the chakras in a gentle way through visualization and mantra.

View

- Start by finding a comfortable position in a place where you won't be disturbed during meditation. A sitting position is better, cross-legged. Keep your back straight.
- Close your eyes and feel the weight of your body on the floor or pillow. Focus only on the weight of the body, the weight of thearti, the feeling of the floor or floor below you. Allow your mind to rest there for a few moments, aware of the solid quality of the earth beneath you.
- Breathe five times deeply. Just inhale, fill the lungs etirate out with a sigh. With each exhalation, one enters into an ever deeper relaxation. Then, let the breath relax naturally and turn your attention to the breath itself. Allow yourself to fully feel your breath. There is a refreshing sensation when it enters the nostrils. The chest rises and falls with breath. Each breath carries vital oxygen to your body, as well as the rejuvenating energy of Prana, the pulse of the universe.
- Give up your erilacca attention completely, then turn your mind inward toward your subtle body. Start by focusing your attention on the root chakra at the base of your spine. It is located in the area of the perineum, near the anus. Rest your consciousness there and feel any energy or feeling you may have in this region. Appreciate the earthly and grounding quality of this chakra.

- Focus your mind on the meaning of *muladhara* for a sense of security and survival. Consider the significance of this in your life, as it could relate to your financial or life situation. Imagine what you would do differently if this chakra were optimally balanced.

- In your mind's eye, imagine a four-petaled red flower made of light where the root chakra is located . Feel your energy at the base of your spine. Visualize the brightest and clearest chakra light, purifying everything that could obscure it and calming any physical or emotional pain you may have on this level.

- Now rest your consciousness slightly on the root chakra, in the sacrum behind the genitals. Allow yourself to feel the energy of the sacral chakra.

- Contemplate the meaning of *svadishthana*, which is connected with sexuality, desire and passion. Relate it to your life, to your sexuality and sensuality. It doesn't have to be sexuality, it can be any sensual pleasure that gives you pleasure, like a good meal. Are you too forgiving? Or repressed? Think about how you would live if you had an optimal relationship with your passions and sensory desires.

- Imagine a six-petaled lotus made of orange light. Feel its pulsating energy. Imagine that the light becomes more intense. It does not necessarily radiate, but the brightness increases. Its fluid and watery quality eliminates all negativity and pain, leaving the chakra clean and bright.

- Shift your attention to the solar plexus chakra , which is located behind the navel region somewhere in the belly. Just rest the entity mlì and feel its energy. Reflect on the meaning of manipura in your life as with the two previous chakras. So imagine a ten-petaled light yellow lotus flower. Turn on the light, making it clearer and brighter. Imagine that its burning energy warms your abdomen and burns any obstructions or imbalances in your willpower, as well as any digestive problems you may have.

- Direct your attention to the center of the chest, to the heart chakra. Feel the warm, warm and tender energy of *anahata* gently resting on your chest. Reflect *on the anahata in a* personal way as before. So imagine that there is a lotus of 12 petals of green light in the position of this chakra. Slowly, the light freezes and looks clearer and brighter. Its windy energy drives away the clouds that obscure your sense of affection and love for others, any negativity or defense mechanism that blocks your sensitivity. This wind clears the clouds and cools any pain or sadness you may feel, leaving you with a generalized sense of kindness and kindness.

- Shift your attention to the throat chakra. Feel any energy located in this area, any tension or relaxation, feel the energy and feel it withoutintanziarla modify it. Reflect on the meaning of the *vishuddha* chakra in your life, for your personal use of the word, is your speech constructive and well regarded? Do you have any inhibitions in expressing yourself? Imagine a sixteen-petaled lotus. It ismade of blue blue light. The light slowly becomes clearer and brighter. Any feeling of lightheadedness dissolves in its wide quality and a sense of openness and relaxation is felt in the throat.

- Then shift your attention to the third eye chakra behind your forehead. Feel the energy of this chakra as it is now. Observe the quality of your thoughts and mind. Is your mind calm or overactive? Clear or boring? Can you imagine that things are true when they are not? Reflexiona on the meaning of *ajña*, your mind, the command center. So imagine a two-petal lotus of deep indigo light located in the position of this chakra. Its light slowly becomes brighter and more intense. The sharpness and clarity of his energy dispels any confusion and pierces the rigidity of clinging to beliefs. His light breaks with illusions, fantasies, disappointments and paranoia.

- Slowly move your consciousness back to the throat chakra, and then to the heart chakra, and so on, to the root chakra. This time you don't need to view anything. He stays only briefly in each chakra and feels his energy. Imagine feeling a sense of balance and peace in every chakra. When you reach the root chak , you feel the weight of your body once again. Allow your mind to return from the subtle body to the raw physical body.

- When you're ready, open your eyes and look around. Don't get up yet. Sit down for a moment, letting your consciousness turn to its normal waking state.

AND THAT'S IT! NOTE that this meditation leaves out any mention of the crown chakra. This is on purpose. Distributing the energy of the crown chakra requires long and patient work on the lower chakras. Any premature attempt to harness their energy could lead to disaster.

Also note that this meditation involves, *in the end*, returning to the root chakra and the body. It begins and ends with the awareness of physicality. This is important, because it keeps you in touch with the solidity of everyday life. Although with the chakras, your spirituality can rise to heavenly heights, it is still important to keep your feet firmly planted on the ground.

Playing lesyllables like seeds

REMEMBER IN THE SECTION on chakras, how each chakra has a mantra or seed syllable associated with it? In this section we will see what it is.

The most famous mantra is the simple sound *Om* or *Aum*, the uncreated and primordial sound of the cosmos that expresses absolute reality. It's inside and it sounds through all things, if you can tune in to its frequency. Similarly, the ancient yogic conception of reality says that certain vocal sounds are tuned to certain levels of experience. So each of the chakras has its own sound, and by reciting or singing its seed syllable, you can connect to its energy.

One way to do this is to sit in meditation, close your eyes and sing the appropriate seed syllable of which chakra you want to work. In this type of practice, you just have to focus your attention on the sound itself. Allow your mind to merge with the sound of the mantra.

You can also recite the syllables of the seeds in combination with the previous meditation. Once you've gotten used to the visualization process, sing the appropriate seed syllable as you imagine the shape and color of the lotus of that chakra. Feel the vibration of sound in your body, moving through the appropriate chakra. You can search for syllables on Youtube if you are not sure of their pronunciation.

For convenient reference, here is a list of the chakras with their associated sounds. All rhyme, except the last one, *Om*:

1. Muladhara: *Lam* (pronounced "lum")
2. Svadishthana: Vam
3. Manipura: Ram
4. Anahata: Yam
5. Vishuddha: Ham
6. Ajña: Om

Essential oils for chakras

THERE ARE COUNTLESS ways to balance the chakras. As I said before, some of them are additional methods. Using essential oils and inciensos won't solve any serious problems, but it can withstand the other types of work you do to balance the chakras.

One way is through aromatherapy. You can burn incense or heat essential oils to promote healthy chakra functioning.

1. For the root chakra, patchouli, vetiver, benzoin and angelica are

useful.

2. For the sacral chakra , try ylang-ylang, jasmine, neroli, and rose.
3. For the solar plexus chakra , there is juniper, rosemary and mint, hyssop and cardamom.
4. For the heart chakra , try using geranium, bergamot, mandarin, rosewood and lemon balm.
5. For the throat chakra, blue chamomile, lemongrass and cypress are refreshing.
6. For the third eye chakra, peppermint, spruce, juniper and thyme are excellent.
7. For the crown chakra, use incense, sandalwood, myrrh, lavender or St. John's wort.

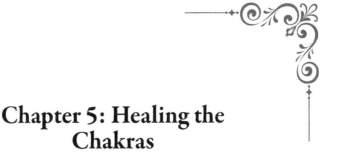

Chapter 5: Healing the Chakras

In the previous chapters, we looked at some of the ways in which the chakras can be balanced. I use some very field and practical things you can do to gain a working knowledge of how the chakras relate to your life. Most of the material has to do with daily activity and going out into the world.

So let's discuss a basic pattern for working with the chakras, for having them open and buzzing.

But some of us may not be prepared for such an approach. Those who have suffered trauma may find that they carry their wounds with them. When an extreme or emotionally impactful event occurs, then the fuse of the chakra can explode. A chakra receives an increase in energy that it is not prepared to receive and short circuits.

Traumas and memories of the past leave their tonality in the chakras, and the chakra goes out, being completely blocked. It is as if the chakra produces a defense shield or protective barrier around it to prevent further injury, such as a hard, impenetrable shell.

That defense shield can be difficult to overcome. If you have suffered trauma related to the root chakra, for example, it will be too scary to jump into activities that make your survival instinct intervene. You are in danger instead of turning off and reliving the trauma, which could only serve to harden the protective layer around that chakra.

In that case, it is best to make a gentle turn and work slowly towards chakra healing. Healing the injured chakras involves calming them down, progressively loosening that hard cover until it slowly begins to give way and becomes flexible.

Discover the problem

THE FIRST THING YOU will want to do when healing your chakras is to identify which chakra, or chakra, you need to work on. This means that you have to think about your problem.

It is not always clear what problem has to do with which chakra. For example, let's say you have a shyness and social anxiety that incapacitates you. It has reached an extreme point where it interferes with your life, your social life, no doubt, maybe even your career. Which chakra does it correspond to?

- Consider the **context** first. When does it come out? If you start to panic and become tense when talking to someone of the opposite sex (or anyone else you might be sexually interested in), then the problem is probably connected to your sacral chakra, which governs sexuality.

Or maybe you've dedicated time and energy to your work, creating value for your company. But it scares you a lot to ask your boss for a raise that you desperately deserve. So the problem has to do with assertion and willpower, connected to the solar plexus chakra .

Maybe you don't feel confident expressing yourself effectively. You want to communicate, but you can't find the right words. So, the problem may have to do with the throat chakra.

- **Also notice what kind of thoughts you have** when your problem arises. Do you worry about the fear of your financial situation, or do you start to panic when you think about finances? Maybe you want to work on healing your root chakra .

When you get emotionally close to someone, do you start to have doubts and suspicions about them? If you are as obsessive as possible, are those doubts rooted in reality? If you are very suspicious and wary of people close to you for no reason, then you will want to consider healing work on the heart chakra.

So pay attention to your mood, and the kind of thoughts that are happening in your head. It will help you understand the nature of the problems that affect you.

- **Also notice the emotions and feelings** that arise. How do you feel when someone close to you shows their love or affection? Do you feel the same emotions in your heart? Are you afraid or uncomfortable? Or apathetic? If something seems wrong to you, we recommend that you work on your cora zón chakra.

How do you feel when the theme of spirituality comes up? Perhaps you have resolved your spiritual beliefs. Do you feel cynical or angry when people express a spiritual point of view? Or maybe uncomfortable? Do you feel guilty about changing the beliefs of others when they are different from your own? These could be signs that the crown chakra needs to be worked.

- **Pay attention to where emotions are recorded in your body**. When your problem arises, you probably feel a flow of energy somewhere in your body. It could be a feeling of sinking into your intestines. Maybe it's a lump in the throat. Or it could be a sensation in the heart area. Wherever energy is activated in your body, these physiological sensations are clues as to which chakra is at play.

Here are some preliminary steps we recommend you take to diagnose the problem. So set aside some time to slow down and think about the above points. Rest, maybe meditate a little, then turn your attention inward and look at yourself. Do not stray from what you see, but investigate honestly and without fear.

You will also want to continue diagnosing your chakra as you go through the following meditations. I have highlighted a few points that you will want to pay close attention to.

In general, it is always a good idea to maintain 10-20% of your awareness in your thoughts, feelings and physiological sensations. Just pay attention to everything that is happening in your body or mind. This will help you make some adjustments and precision adjustments on the fly when appropriate.

A meditation to heal the wounded chakras

1. Find a comfortable place, such as a bed or a sofa, where you are not disturbed.
2. Lie on your back and close your eyes. You may prefer to bend your knees and keep your feet flat on the ground.
3. It completely relaxes your body, starting from the muscles of the head and face, downwards or up to the neck, shoulders and then arms. Then relax the upper back and chest. After that, the lower back and abdomen. Then progressively relaxes the groin, legs and feet.
4. Breathing slowly, pay your attention to the prayer. Count from 1 to 7, resting your mind on the aspiration and expiration each time. When you reach 7, start again from 1. Do this several times, until your mind relaxes in an expansive and meditative state.

IF YOUR MIND MOVES away from the breath, that's not a problem. Simply gently bring your attention back to your breathing, letting your mind rest with the gentle rise and fall of your breath.

You may have some other meditation technique to get into that meditative zone of rest and healing. If you prefer to use it at this point, no problem. The idea is simply to make your consciousness expansive and meditative. So use everything that works for you.

1. Now bring to mind the wound that hurts you, whatever the internal wound you need to heal. Do not dwell so much on it or think about it so much, like taking a crust with your mind. He only feels the pain and emotion that comes with it.

Get an idea of how it is and how it feels, without accepting it or rejecting it as something good or bad. Sometimes, just getting carried away by the pain in this way can begin the healing process.

1. Once you have allowed yourself to feel your pain directly, without judgment, direct your attention to the manifestation of energy in the body: Where in the body do you feel sensations related to emotions? Does the energy move or does it stay in one place? Is it hot or cold? Brim? What other qualities does it possess?
2. Feeling the energy in the body can help you locate the chakra you need to heal, as well as all the peripheral areas connected to that wound. Try to feel, physiologically and energetically, the knot, tension or defensive cover that has accumulated around the chakra. Examine it gently with your mind, to get an idea of how hard or soft, firm or yielding, and so on.
3. Visualize your higher power in the space above you. If you are religious, you may want to imagine a figure of your religion. You can imagine your holy guardian angel or someone else. If you prefer, you can visualize your higher power in another way, such as a sphere of white light, for example. If you are not religious, think of him as your most intimate being in a visible way.
4. From your higher power comes a ray of light that touches your

wounded chakra. The color of the light is the same as the color of the chakra. If you are healing your heart chakra, the light will be green. If it is the sacral chakra, the light will be orange and so on.

5. Imagine the light slowly penetrating the chakra. If the chakra energy is warm, the light will have a refreshing cooling effect. If the energy of the chakra is cold, the light will gently warm it. Slowly begin to dissolve the cover surrounding the chakra. Slowly untie the energetic knots come together and repress the energy of that chakra. It also gently heals any wounds and dissolves physical and emotional pain.

All the pain and negativity comes out of the body like a black oozing and pours into the ground, sinking into the earth. Allow yourself to really feel the pain and wound that slowly heal and subside. It's like you have a nightmare and now you're waking up.

Let the light take its time to do its healing work. There is no need to rushthis part of meditation, it gives enough time for healing to do a complete job.

1. Once you feel healed, silently thank your higher power for healing you. You may want to recite a prayer of thanksgiving in your mind, or you may want to silently join your palms in front of you as a sign of respect.

2. Just rest on the feeling of relief, happiness, love or any positive emotion you are experiencing. Do not try to maintain or prolong the feeling, in particular. Let it be, let your mind relax in that state. Stay there as long as you want, enjoying only the reassuring goodness of that positive state.

3. After some time, your mind will naturally want to return to the outside world of the new. When you start doing this, open your eyes. Continue to lie down for two or three minutes, simply breathing and remaining aware of the environment around you,

the space between objects, the quality of light.

4. When you're ready, get up from your reclining position. Carry out your daily activities slowly and easily.

I say do things slowly because the new healed chakra is sensitive, so you will want to avoid bringing too much energy into your system too quickly. It is better to do simple tasks and grounding, wash dishes, bathe, and so on. Avoid screens; laptops and phones bring too much power to the head. It is best to keep the energy rooted.

Closing the channel

THE PREVIOUS MEDITATION exercise was a kind of treatment for chakra healing. It focuses on a problem area to dissolve acute trauma in the chakras. But what if you're looking for a more holistic approach that works on the seven chakras?

Following the meditation is a good way to work gently on the healing of each chakra one by one, starting from the root chakra and working all the way to the crown.

One of its main advantages is that it isolates the circuits between the chakras, so that the ergía of prana is not free to move between the root and the crown. This reduces the risk of the kundalini waking up before you are ready for it. If your chakras need this kind of healing, you don't want to open a continuous circuit from the bottom up. This would ruin the entire system. So this meditation isolates prana in each circuit before opening the next.

Think of it as a series of canal locks, like in the Panama Canal. When one gate opens, the other closes behind it. This allows the energy to move incrementally, one circuit at a time. Don't worry, the analogy will make sense the moment we delve into the details of meditation.

1. Lie down as before, on your back with your knees bent and together, your feet resting on the floor.

2. Relax your body, starting from the crown of the head and finding its way through the muscles of the face and jaw, neck, shoulders, back, chest, arms, torso, groin, piernas and feet. You feel correctly that the tension in each area is relieved and dissolved.

3. Use your focus on the breath or any other meditation technique you prefer, relax in a state of calm mind, where your consciousness is calm, but calm and alert. This is the "weak point" of the meditative calm that allows healing.

4. Breathe deeply into the perineum or root chakra like a bellows, filling the site with prana. Exhale again and imagine any negative energy coming out of your nostrils.

As you do this, squeeze the groin muscles to stimulate the root chakra. Breathe in and out of your root chakra, until you feel that it is clear and any negatividad is expelled. Do this several times. With each exhalation, he sings the syllable *lam* (pronounced "lum"), the mantra of the root chakra, letting it resonate and vibrate in the chakra.

1. At your next inhalation, imagine that your inspiration draws energy from the root chakra in the sacral chakra. Hold your breath for only a second or two, keeping the energy in the sacral chakra and allowing it to cover the chakra. Then, as you exhale, the energy circulates back to the root chakra.

Maintain the energy cycle between the root chakra and the sacral chakra several times. This establishes a circuit between the two chakras, as if electricity were passing through them. As you exhale, sing the syllable *vam*, the mantra of the sacral chakra, and feeliche vibrate through that chakra.

Keep repeating this until the energy begins to move effortlessly on its own and dissolves any wounds or scars on the chakras.

1. Then, in the next inspiration, pull prana from the root chakra to the solar plexus chakra. Once again hold your breath for a moment, allowing it to penetrate and loosen the chakra. Then exhale, bringing the prana back to the root chakra. Repeat the cycle several times until it feels natural.

Then inhale the prana into the solar plexus and close the root chakra to reduce the circuit, so that the energy moves between the sacral chakra and the solar plexus chakra. Keep repeating that circuit, lift the prana with inspiration and lower it with the exhale. Do this until the energy circulates quite easily and effortlessly. With each exhalation, he sings the syllable ram, the mantra of the solar plexus chakra .

1. Now increase the circuit again, attracting energy from the sacral chakra into the corazón chakra with your inhalation. Let it circulate through the three chakras for some time. Then, in the last breath, hold it in the heart chakra and close the sacral chakra.

Exhale and bring energy to the solar plexus. It continues to circulate between the heart chakra and the solar plexus. With each exhalation, he sings the syllable yam, from the heart chakra.

1. Then again it widens the circuit, carrying the energy inside the throat chakra in inhalation. Let it circulate from the throat chakra to the solar plexus several times, then reduce the circuit again, so that the energycircles between the throat chakra and the heart chakra. Sing the syllable *ham*, from the throat chakra.
2. Then, it pulls the energy from the heart chakra to the third eye. Circle it several times. Then close the heart chakra and let it circulate between the third eye and the throat chakra until it feels natural and effortless. As you exhale, chant *om*, the mantra of the third eye chakra.

3. Then it widens the circuit so that the energy moves between the throat chakra and the crown chakra . It allows them to move several times between them, so it closes the throat chakra and reduces the circuit to the third eye chakras and the crown chakra. Continue to breathe as before, pulling the energy upwards when you inhale and lowering it when exhaling.

4. This next part is a crucial step, which you should not skip. Once the energy has circulated between the third eye chakra and the crown chakra, it widens the circuit again by opening the throat chakra in a new way. Then it reduces the circuit to the throat chakra and the third eye.

5. Just as you climbed the chakra ladder, progressively increasing and reducing each circuit, you will now descend, until the energy returns to circulate between the sacral chakra and the root.

6. Finally, close the chakra and breathe energy several times in and out of the root chakra. As you went up and down the seven chakra ladder, it could be that prana caught some negativity in its journey. Now that it is back at the level of the root chakra, you can expel it. Just exhálla and imagine that you leave your body completely, leaving your subtle energy system clean and clear.

7. Continue to lie down for a while, resting only your mind and body. In this and in all meditation exercises, write down how you feel next. Do you feel rested? Purified? Do you feel more or less negative emotions? Or do you feel the same?

Your feelings are indications of which practices are benefiting or hurting you, or sixthi wasting your time. But don't let this discourage you from continuing a practice. Sometimes you have to continue with this for some time before you start noticing the effects.

1. After giving yourself some time, when your thoughts beginto

return to your outside world, open your eyes. Let yourself adjust a little. So get up and resume your daily activities with awareness.

As in a system of canal locks, the locks or doors are not all open at once, so in this meditation, the chakras are only selectively opened. This allows prana to circulate only between two or three chakras at a time. This creates closed limited circuits. This denies the danger of opening a complete circuit from the root to the crown, which could cause the kundalini to rise prematurely.

Remember that there are two stages in this meditation: first, to increase energy, step by step, from the root to the crown; and secondly, pull it back to the rail, step by step.

The second phase is fundamental. It supports you by bringing energy back into the realm of daily manifestation. You cannot always be in the crown chakra or take permanent vacations in the spiritual realm. You must bring back to solid earth, to the world of daily activity.

The second stage also allows you to clean up any residue that prana collected when you pushed and pulled it through the chakras. This purifies the chakras and puts them in harmony with each other. It also facilitates healing. Even a small cut is prone to an infection, which must be treated and treated. Only then, when the chakras undergo trauma, the negative energy accumulates and vanishes. This meditation helps to eliminate negative energy.

Healing the chakras with herbs

I'M SURE YOU KNOW THAT old proverb: an ounce of prevention is worth a pound of care. But if you already need a cure, sometimes the best remedy is not quick action, but slow and gentle. The above meditations can be too direct and aggressive in approach. Fortunately there are more gentle methods.

For millennia, the medical science of Ayurveda has been practiced in India as a way to heal the body and promote a holistic and preventive approach to the health of body and mind. Ayurveda deals in part with the energy of the body and is an excellent complement to the practices that work with the chakras and the subtle energy system.

Various herbs resonate with the energy of some chakras and can be used to heal and balance them. I will give you some options for each chakra, because some of these herbs may be difficult to find where you live. This applies especially to Ayurvedic drugs, which may not be available in stores.

1. Herbs for the root chakra

Ayurvedic: A great Ayurvedic herb to remedy problems with the root chakra is **shilajit**. Shilajit is a rather strange supplement, but it is very powerful and beneficial. It is a dark brown or black, tarry substance that flows between the rocks of the Himalayas. It is also found in the Caucasus and Altai mountain ranges.

As the Indian tectonic plate pushed against the Eurasian plate, it caused it to bend the earth, lifting the great Himalayan mountain range. In the process, a lot of plant matter and plants were swallowed up by the rocks. Over long centuries, it has been transformed into the powerful tarry substance shilajit.

Shilajit is full of minerals, vitamins, amino acids and many natural compounds that are essential for good health. You can detach a small portion the size of a phosphorus head and mix it with warm milk or drinking water.

If you can fool the shilajit enco ntrar, the purest quality freezes when it's cold and becomes lush when it's hot. You can check the quality by burning a small portion. If it expands and turns into ash bubbles, it is pure.

General: Other herbs that help to heal and balance the root chakra are cloves, dandelion, horseradish and pepper. Root vegetables, such as potatoes and carrots, also support the root chakra. As these vegetables grow underground, they have an earthy, grounded energy that resonates with the root chakra.

2. Herbs for the sacral chakra

Ayurvedic: A well-known aphrodisiac, **ashwagandha** (meaning, literally, "horse smell") has a reputation for "Hindu viagra," but has many more tricks in the manga than regulating sexual desire. Ashwagandha is a root that is usually ground and taken in capsule form. It increases the overall energy level, including, yes, libido, but it also strengthens the immune system and helps regulate mood. In particular, it stabilizes serotonin levels, lowering them if they are too high and increasing them if they are too low. Since low serotonin is associated with anxiety and depression, ashwagandha is a great herb for treating these problems. It also regulates the stress hormone cortisol.

General: Calendula is an herb that helps heal the sacral chakra and promotes creativity. Other beneficial herbs are sandalwood, coriander, fennel, gardenia, cinnamon and vanilla. Foods that promote healthy chakra function include meat, eggs, beans, and nuts.

3. Herbs for solar plexus chakra

Ayurvedic: **Turmeric** is a common element in any Hindu cuisine, but it is also an excellent home remedy and Ayurvedic medicine in its own right. The solar plexus chakra, manipura, is connected to willpower and also to digestive fire. Turmeric promotes healthy digestion by calming or estimating the digestive focus of the solar plexus chakra as needed. It also helps reduce depression, which can decrease your willpower.

Turmeric often comes in powder form. You can mix it with water and drink it. One of turmeric twice a day promotes good digestion. Some even swear that it cures the symptoms of depression.

General: Mint, jasmine, lavender, rose, basil and ginger help heal the solar plexus chakra . Pine pollen is also a powerful healing agent for the solar plexus chakra. It is full of DHEA, a substance that the body produces naturally. It improves the adrenal glands and the endocrine system. It promotes self-confidence and willpower. Digestion also improves.

4. Herbs for the heart chakra

Ayurvedic: We have already mentioned ashwagandha as an herb to heal the sacral chakra. Well, it is also of great help to the heart chakra. Another herb that calms and heals the heart chakra es **shatavari**. Shatavari is a tonic for general health, which is also used specifically to support the female reproductive system. Here we are more interested in how it stimulates the healthy functioning of the heart and supports the activity of the heart chakra.

It can be taken as a powder, in capsule form or as a liquid. If you take it as a powder, you can mix it with clarified butter. In that case, it is useful to heat it with clarified butter to help release its healing properties.

Gene Eral: Hawthorn berry, rose and thyme help heal the heart chakra . The hawthorn berry has healing properties especially for the heart and helps treat heart problems such as arrhythmia and blood pressure. It is also a potentitioxidant. It reduces stress and anxiety and promotes an emotional sense of well-being and love.

5. Herbs for the throat chakra

Ayurvedic: The throat chakra or *vishuddha* is connected to the thyroid gland. Any herbace that is used to treat thyroid disorders is also useful for healing the throat chakra. The Ayurvedic formula **kanchanaraguggulu** is a powerful remedy for problems with the thyroid gland. Removes stagnant phlegm from the tissues of the body.

Also in resonance with the throat chakra is the **brahmi**. Brahmi is an herb that promotes concentration and cognitive functioning in general, and language and language in particular. It is an excellent remedy for problems affecting the throat chakra.

General: Peppermint, salt and lemongrass are good herbs to treat throat chakras problems. Slippery elm can also be used to treat inflammation and irritation of the throat. A sufficient level of iodine in the body is indispensable for thyroid health. Algae are full of iodine, as are many other nutrients that are often lacking in immodern diets.

6. Herbs for the Third Eye Chakra

Ayurvedic: The third eye chakra is connected to the pineal gland and the higher functions of the brain. **Gotu Cola** is apode of pink Ayurvedic herbs to heal and improve this chakra. It increases the absorption of oxygen in the cells of the body, and in particular and especially in the brain. It also thickens the colossus body, or tissue that connects the left hemisphere and the tenth hemisphere of the brain. This increases communication between hemispheres and leads to an integration of intuitive and rational, holistic and linear thinking styles. It also brings the right and left channels – ida and pingala – in harmony.

Meditators especially benefit from the use of this herb. It has been shown to increase long-term intelligence.

General: In addition to mugwort, poppy, rosemary and lavender, passionflower is used to treat disorders of the third eye chakra. It treats insomnia, depression, anxiety and headaches and improves mental clarity and cognition.

7. Herbs for the Crown Chakra

Ayurvedic: The crown chakra is more rarefied and abstract than the other chakras. It is part of the subtle body system, but it is above and outside the body. It acts as a portal between the worldly and spiritual planes of our existence. So you need an herb with a more subtle action.

Brahmi, mentioned above, generally moves intelligence (and even hair growth) and works to heal the crown chakra. **Gotu kola** also works to heal this spiritual chakra. Both herbs help concentration and clarity, allowing you to rise to levels more than meditation cough.

There is also **shankhpushpi**. It reduces stress and keeps the mind in a relaxed, calm and focused state. Improves memory and stimulates sleep. In general, it induces a sense of peace and spiritual well-being.

General: Coloring herbs, such as sage, help purify the energy in the crown chakra, which facilitates better communication between the physical and spiritual parts of our being. In particular, sage has been shown to increase sensory clarity, memory, healthy brain function and intelligence.

Also useful is lavender, which increases clarity, reduces anxiety, relieves the nervous system and reduces depression. It also contains several antioxidant compounds.

A word of farewell

He insisted again and again on the dangers of jumping in practice without doing the right basic work, because I want to make sure that the message hits home with hammers. The dangers are real and the scene of spirituality is full of people who have brought to themselves unnecessary suffering with their reckless negligence. These warnings should not be taken as a discouragement from engaging in spiritual practice, but as an encouragement to enter it with caution and with the guidance of someone who knows what they are doing.

Ever since Eastern spirituality first burst onto the Western scene in a big way in the 60s, the word "guru" has been poisoned by its frequent abuse. A master of oral espionage does not have to be a cult leader or a cunning man of God. The Sanskrit word "guru" means "heavy", because an authentic guru is heavy with good qualities. So avoid bad gurus like the plague and look for a guide whose true interest is in the spiritual growth of his students.

Now you know enough about the chakras to begin with. My hope for you is that you will use the information contained in this book to explore your subtle body and mind safely, find self-healing, and develop your spiritual practice into something deep and nourishing for your life.

Finally, if you liked this book, I would like to ask you a favor. Would you be kind enough to share your thoughts and post a review of this book on Amazon? You could also let me know what you would like to see in the next editions of this book.

Your voice is important for this book to reach as many people as possible. The more reviews this book gets, the more people will be able to find it egoding about the incredible benefits of awakening their chakras.

CPSIA information can be obtained
at www.ICGtesting.com
Printed in the USA
BVHW080940090822
644144BV00006B/237